MW01103594

We Build a Drone

Following Instructions

Leonard Clasky

COMPUTER KIDS
Powered by Computational Thinking

PowerKiDS press.

Published in 2018 by The Rosen Publishing Group, Inc.
29 East 21st Street, New York, NY 10010

Book Design: Jennifer Ryder-Talbot
Editor: Caitie McAneney

Photo Credits: Cover, p. 5, 6-7 Dmitry Kalinovsky/Shutterstock.com;
p. 8, 10 Viacheslav Lopatin/Shutterstock.com; p. 12-13, 14 Paolo De Gasperis/
Shutterstock.com; p. 16 marekuliasz/Shutterstock.com; p. 18 Aleksandar Grozdanovski/
Shutterstock.com; p. 21 (remote control) Basyn/Shutterstock.com.

Library of Congress Cataloging-in-Publication Data

Names: Clasky, Leonard.
Title: We build a drone: following instructions / Leonard Clasky.
Description: New York : Rosen Classroom, 2018. | Series: Computer Kids: Powered by
Computational Thinking | Includes glossary and index.
Identifiers: LCCN ISBN 9781538353103 (pbk.) | ISBN 9781538324394 (library bound) |
ISBN 9781538355534 (6 pack) | ISBN 9781538352830 (ebook)
Subjects: LCSH: Drone aircraft--Juvenile literature.
Classification: LCC TL685.35 C53 2018 | DDC 629.133'39--dc23

Manufactured in the United States of America

CPSIA Compliance Information: Batch #WS18RC: For Further Information contact Rosen Publishing, New York, New York at 1-800-237-9932

Table of Contents

You Can Build Anything!

Have you ever built something using instructions? Some people like to build model airplanes or ships from kits. Other people like to build birdhouses or tree forts out of wood. Is it possible for a person to build something more **complex**, like a robot or drone?

Robots and drones are both machines that complete a task according to human command. Some are programmed to **automatically** do a task, while others are operated by **remote control**. Drones are also called unmanned aerial vehicles (UAVs). They fly through the sky, guided by human command. These machines are complex, but they aren't impossible to make yourself. You can build anything as long as you have the right parts, clear instructions, and **persistence**!

You can fly your drone high into the sky!

What Is a Drone?

There are many different kinds of drones in the world. Some are as big as airplanes. They are used by the military in times of war. Some are so small they can fit in the palm of your hand.

Drones can fly over an area, taking photographs from above.

Drones are used for many different reasons. The U.S. military uses drones to complete missions that would be unsafe for pilots. Wildlife **experts** use drones to study animal populations and movement. Some groups use drones to find missing people or track a storm. Drones can deliver water, food, and medicine to people who are stuck somewhere out of reach. Many drones have cameras and **sensors** that can record photographs, videos, and data. Sometimes regular people fly drones recreationally, or just for fun!

This kit comes with the frame already assembled.
Other kits have more parts that have to be put together.

Drone Kits

Now that you know about drones, you might want to build your own. There are several ways to go about this challenge. You might build the drone completely from scratch. You'll need to assemble all of the correct parts and have a deep knowledge of how parts work together.

If you're just starting out, it might be helpful to buy a drone kit. Kits have all the necessary parts for a drone. Some drones are bought ready to fly. Others have to be assembled. Assembling a drone kit is a great way to learn about how the different parts work together to keep a machine up in the air. The most important part of the kit is the instruction **manual**!

The Frame

Drones come in all shapes and sizes. You'll want to **research** the different drone frames before you choose your drone.

Quadcopter drones are some of the most popular recreational drone styles. Quadcopter drones have a frame shaped like an "x" with four propellers. Other drone frames have three, six, or eight arms on them. If you're a beginner, a quadcopter is a great choice. It's a simple frame and easy to use. Your kit may come with a bottom board and four arms that are not yet attached. You may have to attach electronic speed controllers, too. These parts allow the flight controller to control the speed and direction of the motors.

Quadcopter drones have four arms, each attached to a motor.

The Motors

What's the next step to putting together your drone? Now that you've chosen your drone frame, it's time to look at the motors. What are motors and why are they necessary?

The small parts of a drone may be hard to put together. It's important to look at instructions and how-to videos online.

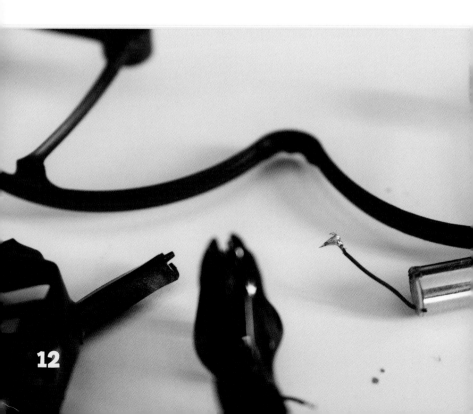

Drones can't fly without motors. Motors are the parts that make a machine work, whether it's a car, robot, or drone. Motors work to get your drone off the ground and into the air. Each propeller needs a motor to make it spin. Each motor should have the same amount of power so the drone flies evenly. If you were building a drone from scratch, you would have to make or buy your motors separately. Attach the motors to the electronic speed controllers.

Propellers come in many different sizes.

Propellers

Next, connect your propellers to the motors. Propellers are long, thin parts that have the ability to rotate quickly. You can attach the propellers to the motors using special parts that come with your kit. As the motor spins, the propellers also spin. The propellers lift the drone off the ground. As their name suggests, they propel the drone, or move it forward. This forward push is called propulsion.

By now, you can probably see how all the parts work together. The propeller is attached to the motor, which is attached to the electronic speed controller. By following directions, you are well on your way to finishing your drone! But what's powering the drone?

Battery

So far, you've chosen your drone's frame, added electronic speed controllers, added motors, and added propellers. What's next in the instruction manual? It's very important to follow the instructions step by step.

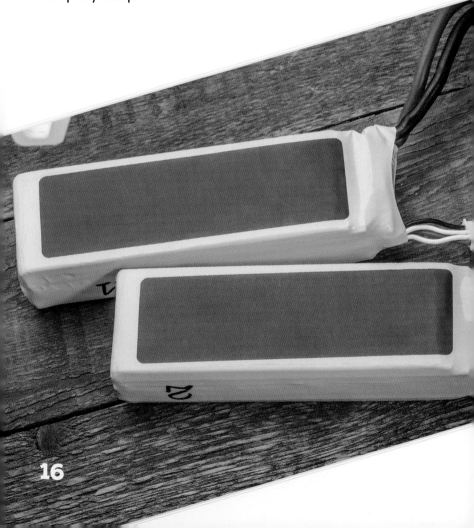

Your next step is to add the power source. Like all electronic machines, drones need a power source in order to make their motor run. Power sources include electricity, solar power, and batteries. While some drones are powered by sunlight, many have batteries. Almost all remote-controlled, recreational drones have lithium polymer batteries. These batteries are lightweight and very powerful. It's also easy to recharge this kind of battery. Attach the battery to your drone. You are one step closer to finishing your drone project!

These lithium polymer batteries can be used to power your drone.

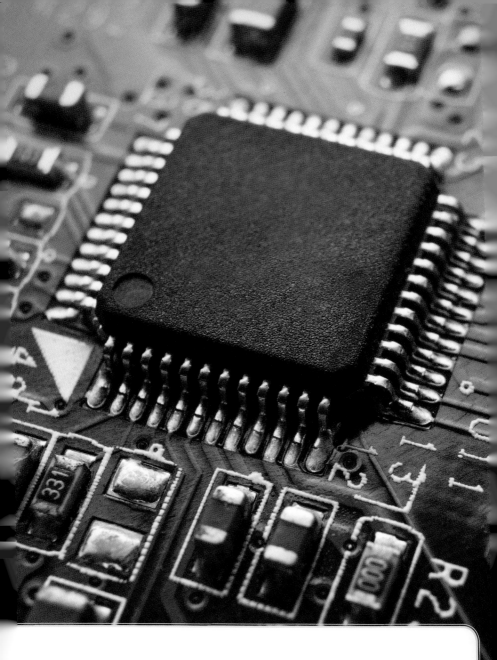

Flight controllers look a bit like circuit boards in computers.

Flight Controller

Now, you have to connect one of the most important parts of the drone—the flight controller. The flight controller is like the drone's brain. It commands the drone to do certain tasks.

Flight controllers have a **microprocessor**, sensors, and parts that receive input and give output. Some important parts of the flight controller are its sensors. Sensors can tell how fast a drone is going, how high it is in the sky, and what direction it is traveling. Some even have a **GPS**, which helps determine exactly where the drone is. The flight controller communicates with the electronic speed controller to move the motor, which moves the propellers. Your drone is almost ready to hit the skies!

Receivers and Transmitters

Your drone has been built! However, you can't fly it yet. You need to make sure the **receiver** and **transmitters** work together. Receivers and transmitters are how remote-controlled electronics work. You send a message from a transmitter on the remote control device to a receiver on the drone.

The receiver channels have to connect to the correct flight controller channels. Programming the flight controller is a difficult task, but if you follow the directions, you should be successful.

remote control

Can you fly your drone yet? There's one more step. You have to register your drone with the Federal Aviation Administration (FAA). The FAA has rules for using drones that you'll have to learn first.

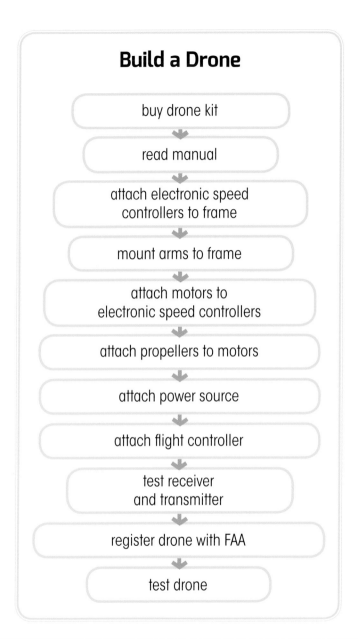

Build a Drone

buy drone kit

read manual

attach electronic speed
controllers to frame

mount arms to frame

attach motors to
electronic speed controllers

attach propellers to motors

attach power source

attach flight controller

test receiver
and transmitter

register drone with FAA

test drone

You can use a flowchart like this one
to help you build your drone.

Testing Your Drone

You have built your drone. You have programmed the flight controller. You have registered with the FAA and learned drone rules. After all of those steps, it is time to test your drone!

Get comfortable with your remote control device and learn what each button makes the drone do. Then, try it out. Did your drone fly? Did it follow the commands from your remote control device the way you planned? If so, you've successfully built your own drone. If your drone did not fly, you have to find out what went wrong. Go back in the instruction manual and see if you missed anything. By following each step correctly, you should be able to have your drone flying in no time!

Glossary

automatic: Having devices that permit operation without help from a person.

complex: Having to do with many parts that work together.

expert: Someone with great knowledge about a certain subject.

GPS: Stands for Global Positioning System. A system that uses satellite signals to locate places on Earth.

manual: A book that gives instructions for something.

microprocessor: The device in a computer that manages information and controls what the computer does.

persistence: The quality of continuing to do something despite challenges.

receiver: A device that receives radio waves.

remote control: Control of operation from a distance, often by radio signal.

research: Studying to find something new.

sensor: A tool that can detect changes in its surroundings.

transmitter: A device that sends out radio waves.

Index